T0228773

This play is dedicated to the 96 men, women and children who lost their lives at Hillsborough and the many thousands more that have been affected by the tragedy.

Jo Halliday and Layla Dowie

BEYOND HILLSBOROUGH

OBERON BOOKS
LONDON

WWW.OBERONBOOKS.COM

First published in 2014 by Oberon Books Ltd
521 Caledonian Road, London N7 9RH
Tel: +44 (0) 20 7607 3637 / Fax: +44 (0) 20 7607 3629
e-mail: info@oberonbooks.com
www.oberonbooks.com

Edit copyright © Jo Halliday and Layla Dowie, 2014

Jo Halliday and Layla Dowie are hereby identified as authors of
this play in accordance with section 77 of the Copyright, Designs
and Patents Act 1988. The authors have asserted their moral
rights.

All rights whatsoever in this play are strictly reserved and
application for performance etc. should be made before
commencement of rehearsal to the authors c/o Oberon Books
Ltd. No performance may be given unless a licence has been
obtained, and no alterations may be made in the title or the text
of the play without the authors' prior written consent.

You may not copy, store, distribute, transmit, reproduce or
otherwise make available this publication (or any part of it) in
any form, or binding or by any means (print, electronic, digital,
optical, mechanical, photocopying, recording or otherwise),
without the prior written permission of the publisher. Any person
who does any unauthorized act in relation to this publication may
be liable to criminal prosecution and civil claims for damages.

A catalogue record for this book is available from the British
Library.

PB ISBN: 978-1-78319-134-5
E ISBN: 978-1-78319-633-3

Visit www.oberonbooks.com to read more about all our books
and to buy them. You will also find features, author interviews and
news of any author events, and you can sign up for e-newsletters
so that you're always first to hear about our new releases.

Contents

Introductions   9
by Stephen Kelly and Sheila Coleman

Beyond Hillsborough   13

Using *Beyond Hillsborough* in the Classroom   57

This play was researched during 2011 and 2012
and written in 2012.

We would like to thank everyone who has helped
and supported us in this research.

We have been overwhelmed by the support of local business,
staff, students and parents from West Kirby Grammar School
and thank them wholeheartedly. Helpful advice was received
from: the staff of the Liverpool Everyman & Playhouse,
playwright Tony Green, and Kevin Sampson. Encouragement
from Max Stafford-Clark and Barney Norris (Out of Joint).

We are particularly grateful for the kindness and generosity
shown by the families and survivors of Hillsborough –
speaking to us, inviting us into their homes, their meetings and
sharing their experiences. Special thanks to Stephen Kelly,
Jenni Hicks, Sheila Coleman, Kenny and Wendy Derbyshire,
Barry Devonshire, Neil Sampson, Rob White, Jimmy
McGovern, Rogan Taylor, Steve Rotherham, Phil Shaw,
Esther McVey, Lesley Rampton, Jo Avison and everyone at
The HJC, HFSG and Hope for Hillsborough.

We have assembled hours of transcripts and unfortunately
only a small amount is directly represented.

Royalties from sales of this book will be shared between the
Hillsborough Justice Campaign, the Hillsborough Family
Support Group and Hope for Hillsborough; all three groups
have been involved in the development of this play.

I first heard about the drama *Beyond Hillsborough* on the local radio. Immediately it came to me that the people involved were young. It was my belief they were future campaign members, people that could carry on to help achieve truth and justice for the 96 victims of Hillsborough and the many thousands left traumatised, due to the cover-up that followed the events of 15 April 1989. Also they would ensure that the message will, and rightly so, stay loud and clear.

I spoke to teachers and students, I then had to be involved; their enthusiasm was infectious – the relationship with family members and survivors was so respectful; you just had to support it.

I first watched the drama at the school, an evening for Hillsborough families, survivors and families of the cast. It was very distressing, yet so well put together. I travelled to Edinburgh to see first-hand how people would react to the drama outside Merseyside. I was shocked, yet pleased at the public response, I was really confident public opinion was with us, and through a group of students in a Quaker House in Edinburgh, my spirits lifted.

My first instinct was right, I watched the cast grow and gel together becoming a unit, I was proud to have been of some help. The cast and crew involved should also be proud of the part they played in putting together a message from young people who listened to us, that message is JUSTICE FOR THE 96. I am really confident they will carry on and support the Hillsborough campaign in the future and bring it to its rightful conclusion.

Stephen Kelly

When Jo Halliday first contacted me in respect of writing a Hillsborough play I was encouraged that she said it would be a verbatim account.

There have been so many lies about the Hillsborough Disaster over the years and people's words have been distorted or edited in a way that has robbed them of validity. This verbatim play was the opportunity to speak the words of families, survivors and campaigners.

I was so impressed with the young students involved, who researched with rigour, and painstakingly strived to accurately emulate the owners of the words. They delivered with honesty, commitment and talent. It genuinely was a pleasure to work with the group.

The authors need to be commended not only for their teaching skills but for choosing the medium of drama to deliver a controversial yet honest account of the views of those immersed in an enduring campaign for truth and justice.

Sheila Coleman
Hillsborough Justice Campaign

Beyond Hillsborough was first performed in 2012 in The Drama Studio, West Kirby; The Lantern Theatre, Liverpool; and The Quaker Meeting House, Edinburgh.

THE COMPANY 2012

Directed by Jo Halliday and Layla Dowie

STEPHEN KELLY	Joe Davies
SHEILA COLEMAN	Ellie Devereux-Roberts
JENNI HICKS	Sarah Browning
ROB WHITE	Jade Thomson
NEIL SAMPSON	Jason Gallantry
FRIEND	Liam Martin
ANNE WILLIAMS / POLICE	Elly Simmons
AMBULANCE WORKER	Jade Thomson
ROGAN TAYLOR	Rach' Jones
STEVE ROTHERHAM	Liam Martin
KENNY DERBYSHIRE	Mattie Warbrick
WENDY DERBYSHIRE	Caz Bagley / Rhianne Robinson Parsons
BRIAN READE	Mattie Warbrick

KEEP IN TOUCH

Follow us on Twitter: Zipped Up Theatre

@ZippedUpTheatre

CHARACTERS

STEPHEN KELLY
his brother Michael died at Hillsborough.
HJC member.

SHEILA COLEMAN
academic researcher. HJC member.

JENNI HICKS
her daughters Sarah and Vicky died at
Hillsborough. HFSG member.

ROB WHITE
Hillsborough survivor.

NEIL SAMPSON
Hillsborough survivor.

FRIEND
writer.

ANNE WILLIAMS
her son Kevin died at Hillsborough. Set up Hope
for Hillsborough.

POLICE
Cheshire Police Officer.

Ambulance Worker TONY EDWARDS, Yorkshire.

ROGAN TAYLOR
journalist and broadcaster.

STEVE ROTHERHAM
Labour MP, Liverpool.

BRIAN READE
Sports journalist, *Daily Mirror*.

KENNY DERBYSHIRE
Hillsborough survivor. HJC member.

WENDY DERBYSHIRE
Hillsborough survivor. HJC member.

As audience enter and take their seats a montage of recorded interview extracts from news reports from 1989 on Hillsborough is played through speaker. Cast enter in blackout, lights come up to show cast staring out, stillness/angst. Lights down, montage of reports again and cast sit SR/SL. Two actors stand DSL/DSR.

ACTOR 1: On the 15 of April 1989 a football match was played between Liverpool and Nottingham Forest, the neutral venue chosen was Hillsborough. Before 1989, Hillsborough was just the name of one of England's famous old football grounds, but for the last 23 years the word, 'Hillsborough', has evoked memories of Britain's worst-ever sporting disaster. Only six minutes into the game – play was stopped when it was realised that spectators on the terraces behind the Liverpool goal had been severely crushed. 96 men, women and children were killed and hundreds of others injured and left permanently traumatised. We'll never know the full extent of the damaging legacy.

ACTOR 2: As Steve Rotherham MP said in the House of Commons, 'there is a fundamental misunderstanding of what happened on the day and in the dark days, weeks, years and ashamedly decades that followed'. Instead of those at fault taking responsibility for their actions, a co-ordinated campaign began to shift the blame and look for scapegoats. To this day nobody has been held accountable for Hillsborough.

ACTOR 1: Using only words from transcribed interviews we are going to present the truth.

Soundtrack of montage, actors sit.

Act 1 – Introductions

Company sit and watch projection on screen in silence. They turn to face projected image of Andy Burnham MP at Hillsborough 20ᵗʰ Memorial at Anfield.

PROJECTION/RECORDING/TREVOR HICKS: I'd just now like to introduce the Right Honourable Andy Burnham, Secretary of State for Culture, Media and Sport.

PROJECTION/RECORDING/ANDY BURNHAM: Remembering any loss of life on this scale is painful, *(Pause.)* it is even harder when a tragedy with no natural disaster but entirely man made. When it involves so many young people *(Pause.)* when those who lost most have suffered so many more dark days *(Pause.)* ever since. Hillsborough left deep wounds that will never heal *(Pause.)* its horror is not demeaned by the passage of time. The TV images are still harrowing to watch, but today as the Prime Minister has asked me to convey, we can at least pledge that 96 fellow football supporters who died will never be forgotten. *(Shout of 'Justice'.)* and he has asked us to think at this time *(Crowd start to cheer, 'Justice for the 96'.)*

Projection ends.

Company chants in conjunction with recording.

MAN enters stage carrying his chair, wearing jeans, black Fred Perry shirt. Places chair DSR, stands behind chair, speaks directly to audience.

ACTOR 1: Stephen Kelly, now 59 years old (he won't thank us for telling you that!). He lost his brother, Michael in the disaster.

ACTOR/S.K: *(He sits.)* Do you want to hear my
Hillsborough story?

Beat.

*WOMAN enters. Middle class. Beige pencil skirt, shirt and cardigan/
jacket, court shoes.*

ACTOR/J.H: Jenni Hicks, her and Trevor – their two
girls, Sarah and Vicky were killed at Hillsborough.
She's an adopted Scouser!

ACTOR/S.K: I was out for a run when it happened. I
lived in Penny Lane. I came home, my then wife,
Christine and I went shopping and there were
mobs of people all looking in windows watching
televisions. What's going on? All this carry on? I
was a taxi driver at the time and knew I'd be going
out to work that night. It was Christine that said,
'what about your Mike?' That's my brother, he's
a red, I'm a blue. The city was flat that day even
though Everton had won. I went home that night
at about 4/5 o'clock. We had a circular table with a
phone on it… The phone rang, it was 'Steve, your
Margaret has phoned and there's no sign of your
Michael yet.' I thought he's probably had a few
pints, no mobiles then or Twitter – none of that
business. I went to bed, went to sleep – but 7am, I
sat bolt upright, woke my wife. I was worried about
our Mike, I thought I should phone me mum, I left
it to 9am to phone me ma to check she was OK.

So I phoned the number given on the TV –
eventually I got through. I spoke to the police and
gave an absolute description; long hair, he'd had an
op 12-18 months before and he had a scar from his
chest bone to his stomach, a fresh scar, still raised.
He wore a ring on his middle finger, I thought it
was weird but I bought it for him for his birthday
so I knew. Sounds weird to say this, but he had
no style whatsoever. The description I gave was

Mike to a tee! They phoned me back and told me not to worry – no one of that description had been identified so I felt OK.

Beat.

ACTOR/J.H: When I lost my girls they were 15 and 19 at the time, they died unnecessarily so there's only myself and Trevor on a personal level to fight for them, they're not here, they've lost their rights, there's only us to fight for them, it's not about me, it's about them. We lived in London at the time of the disaster, I mean the girls were brought up on football, they were keen Liverpool supporters you know, we were all season ticket holders at Anfield. Vicky was 15 but she was going to be 16 in the July, she was you know GCSE age, in fact she was going to do them next week. I think she had her French oral the middle of the week that she died, anyhow Sarah had been up at university in Liverpool since September so she'd only been out of Sixth Form college for months. She was 19 on the Monday and she died on the Saturday.

Beat.

There were, you know, survivors in the pens who remembered Sarah and Vicky and where they were. There were these two young guys and obviously Sarah and Vicky were just teenage girls at the time and erm, they said, 'Oh we went...' – they're describing their day and how they got there and they go into the pen and they said, 'we saw these two girls, who we now realised were the Hicks' sisters and we thought, 'ooh our luck's in! cos we were standing next to them' *(Pause.)* I, it's, the disaster seems like yesterday and yet...it seems a million miles away as well, so it's a very strange thing...very, very difficult thing. It seems like yesterday but seems like *(Breathes in heavily.)* yonks since I've seen the girls...so there's the dichotomy it, it's a dual thing this time thing. It's a long time, but it's, it some ways it's, it's flown over. Just keep saying...I keep asking, 'What have I been doing for 23 years? Where has 23 years gone?' *(Pause.)* Well I'm the Vice Chairman of the Hillsborough Family Support Group, I've been involved in that right from the start, we were founded in the July of 1989 solely for the bereaved families, it started with next of kins and now there's over seventy families that are part of our group so that's a lot of people, so there's a lot going on with that, organsising an', I'm also on the subcommittee for the release of the documents, er and I've got a job and ha ha – I only work part-time ermm and Marks and Spencers were fantastic – if I need to go to London for meetings they'd change my days in work. Yeh, ermm and Trevor, he runs his own company, he's remarried and got a new family and everything erm...but I, I do have other things as well.

Actors look across at each other. Beat.

ACTOR/S.K: To be fair I was getting a bit panicked... so I said to Christine, I thought sod it, I'm going, so I drove down to Leppings Lane gates in a little red Nissan Micra. It was a really warm day, dead sunny, but there was a policeman stood in front of the gates in a big overcoat, when I pulled up to the gates he said... and I don't mean to be rude, 'Fuck off'. I told him no and said me brother's missing, he said, 'I've told you, I've fucking told ya', so I took me keys out of the car and threw them over the gate. Then all hell's let loose and he arrested me.

ACTOR/J.H: The way Trevor and I were treated that night, the questions we were asked when the police interviewed us. Straight away it was about drink. 'Did you stop at a pub on the way?' And er...we said we had a picnic! 'Did you have wine with your picnic?' We felt like we were being interrogated, 'you know, it was all about alcohol…so the mindset was there… Right from the very start. Erm… it opened my eyes about the police and things. I suppose I was very naïve because I came from a generation where erm…and I brought the girls up in the same way, the police were there to protect us. We weren't police haters.

ACTOR/S.K: That's really when the nightmare started. Proved how badly all of us were treated. They made me sit there for hours watching this tape to identify Mike. The bastards – they made me watch him die! I think of that every day. *(Pause.)* I got taken to identify him and *(He stands.)* I'm standing in front of this velvet curtain and it opens with no warning, I fall back and I'm straining to see, he had a purple shroud over him, and I think, 'Oh no, obviously it was our Mike'. I said, 'Can I go and see him?', and they said 'No, he's the property of the coroner now!' I said, 'he's the property of me Ma.' *(Silence.)* You didn't know how much your life was never going to be the same, three years later, I didn't have a job, I was homeless and I'd split up with my wife. You never realised how it was going to affect you.

Female actor enters. Smartly dressed, glasses, dark colours.

ACTOR 3: Sheila Coleman, former lecturer in Higher Education. Originally employed as an academic researcher to monitor the legal proceedings that followed the disaster.

ACTOR/S.K: Sheila, she's like the spokesperson, the legal person – really speaking she's the only one that does it full time, she's voluntary, she does all the hard work!

ACTOR/S.C: I've worked with families for so many years, I feel I know a number of the dead and obviously I've never met them but I've sat and I've listened to the stories. But what I found in the main was that…people were just desperate to, to talk and basically I think, I realise now, they weren't being treated very nice and they were coming up against brick walls, so the fact that you showed an interest in wanting to know erm people put a lot of trust in you. I come from a background where… I've always had a strong sense of right and wrong, and I often wonder where that comes from, but I actually think it probably stems from being brought up a Catholic. What I saw over the Hillsborough thing, was just this real sense of lies being told and I'm sitting in court – thinking woahh this is wrong and watching it all being done with a veneer of respectability and thinking these people are being exploited in their grief, their vulnerability being exploited… *(Pause.)* We've been to court a couple of times, what with The Taylor Report, the Interim Report and the Stuart Smith stitch-up – but it's a farce…

We're not about targeting individuals saying this police officer and that police officer. You can say that David Duckenfield, the chief superintendent in charge on that day was in overall control and he lost control.

ACTOR/S.K: Erm…I mean we've heard stories over the years about how the fans were blamed er and y'know, it's just totally untrue – an' we need to clear their names.

All three leave and return to sit at side.

KENNY enters. Looks directly at the audience. WENDY enters from other side. She smiles at the audience.

KENNY: I'm Kenny…this is Wendy, she's me er…me wife.

WENDY: We met because of Hillsborough.

KENNY: We both were there. I was in Leppings Lane
and Wendy was sat above.

WENDY: So Kenny was experiencing it and I was
observing it. We didn't meet until ten years after the
disaster.

KENNY: Me and Wendy, we met through the campaign.
We've both always been strong believers in the
fight for justice…that's how we met. We started off
as friends…and yanno Wendy was with someone
else be-before she met me and unfortunately her
husband passed away *(Pause.)* and when he passed
away we just got closer and closer.

WENDY giggles.

*A retired Police(wo)man and ex-ambulance worker has entered,
plain clothes – stands and watches.*

POLICE: It was April '89 wasn't it? At that time I'd been
in the police for nine years, I joined in 1980. I'd just
come off a years' secondment to CID. I was on a
2-10 shift. I was er – taking a probationer, I don't
remember his name, on vehicle patrol, general
policing for everyday public order problems based
in Ellesmere Port. As you know it's the Liverpool
overspill, bit like Runcorn and Winsford with the
overspill from the 70s. I would have been in work
at 2 – the other big game that day was Everton v
Norwich, I'm an Evertonian and the match was in
Birmingham and I was disappointed that I couldn't
go. My concentration was on the Everton match
and not on police work. It was Duty 2, paraded on,
updated and went out on patrol. I know for definite
that the person with me had never given a death
message, I'd done many, hardest things particularly
when it's a youngster, there isn't a right or wrong
way. I based it on – don't beat about the bush, you
can deliberate but eventually you just have to say
it. Ironically that day I'd delivered another death

message – but because I was working I didn't even
know what was going on at Hillsborough.

*During speech on 'Ironically' an ex-ambulance worker enters and
stands USL – black and white photograph projections through the
speech of the event.*

AMBULANCE WORKER: Working on the ambulances
we had no idea what we were going to. We started
the day picking up patients for transfer to hospital.
We were diverted to Hillsborough when it came
over the radio that there had been a fatality at the
stadium, but we didn't think anything of that. It
could have been a heart attack or something. Our
boss met us and told there were casualties at the far
end. We were to drive on and help. But the police
wouldn't let us. Our boss reached into the cab,
switched on our horns and said, 'drive on that pitch
and don't stop till you reach the far end'. The first
thing we saw was a group of Liverpool fans running
towards us using ad hoarding, the type you see
round the stadium as a stretcher. There was a body
on it and he had his T-shirt over his face. I thought
that guy's dead. Then we noticed police had put
a cordon halfway up the pitch but there was a
gap – I can still remember how the sound changed
when we drove through – the singing of the Forest
fans at one end gave way to this disjointed sound
of screaming and panic, echoing like the noise in
a swimming pool. *(Pause.)* The vehicle and crew
were swamped by desperate fans begging for help.
We were the only ambulance that was allowed on
the pitch…there were loads of ambulances waiting
outside, they just weren't allowed in. Why were
the other 42 ambulances kept off the pitch? I don't
believe these questions have been answered, even
after all this time. I looked around trying to find
people we could help, I saw a man doing CPR on
a young girl, I said, 'Let's get her'. By the time we

got to the ambulance and looked down – it was a different girl. We'd taken the wrong one. They were sisters, aged 15 and 19 and they both died. That's what gets me the most, I might have saved one of them.

POLICE: Used to have a refreshment break at 5 o'clock, we were just going back out when the Sgt briefed us on events, we had got the information that two of the suspected deaths from Hillsborough lived in Ellesmere Port, it's ages ago – can't think of their names. We were to give them a message, not a death message per se as the individuals hadn't been positively identified. Brief was, suspect, 16 gone with mates, suspected he died at football, been crushed. We needed a member of the family, preferably a parent to go to Sheffield to ID as soon as. Fairly vague, usual for it to be vague, especially when death outside of town. We went directly to the address, it wasn't far, just in Ellesmere Port, a terrace house. This sounds strange but as I'd already delivered a death message that day it had given me confidence – it takes the adrenalin away, there was an air of confidence about me. At that stage the enormity of the events was not known, I didn't see it as a massive event.

AMBULANCE WORKER: I know I'll always blame myself, that won't go away, counselling can't get rid of that.

Images go off.

POLICE: Thinking back now our treatment of them was pretty appalling – we'd have only been with them 10 minutes. We just went from one job to another. I didn't have a reaction, in those days you just got on with it, you didn't question it, you didn't have the traumatic response teams like now. In fact then no support – it was horrendous. I'm sorry, I don't remember any more.

Act 2 – The Meeting

Actors come forward and place their chairs in a semi-circle facing the audience. There is general muttering/mumbling as they enter. One man, KENNY is making tea for the meeting. SHEILA COLEMAN, KENNY and WENDY, JENNI HICKS, JENNI'S FRIEND, ANNE WILLIAMS, NEIL SAMPSON, ROB WHITE.

JENNI: Hi, hope you don't mind, I've brought my friend – he's like an honorary member of the support group, but he's gotta leave a bit early. Is that ok?

FRIEND: Yeah, about 8 ish, sorry about that.

SHEILA: Alright Kenny, you ok? *(General acknowledgements/nods, etc.)*

So first of all I'd like to thank everyone for coming and just to say that we have a lot to get through, errr, I've just written a few things down, I'll have to apologise for my voice because, this is good actually, but it wasn't, it's been errr gone so, been struggling a bit. Errm these are the things I – the monument, update on the panel… Oh and I'd like to introduce you all to Rob White and Neil Sampson, both were at Hillsborough.

Actor (STEPHEN KELLY) enters, looking flustered.

STEPHEN: Sorry I'm late everyone. *(Nods and acknowledges group, audience.)*

KENNY: Alright Steve, do you want a cup of tea?

STEPHEN: Y'alright – er whatever – yeah. Have you told them about Rotterdam, Kenny? – it was brilliant, fundraising.

SHEILA: The main purpose of tonight's meeting is to help yous *(Looks/indicates audience.)* understand where we are up to. To offer the truth...

FRIEND: Well the truth of Hillsborough was the park incident. Do you know that? In the early part of 1989 a young copper was called out at night to a park in Sheffield. Masked men appeared from out of the bushes and put a gun to his head. The young copper nearly died of fright. The men removed their masks, they were police officers. It was all a sort of joke.

Beat.

SHEILA has stood, she's goes to get a drink.

Unfortunately the young copper had a senior copper as a father, he kicked off, it went to Douglas Hurd, the Home Secretary. Hurd got on the blower to the chief constable and said kick arse, erm sack the men involved and move their senior officer...a guy called Mole, a really well-respected, senior copper...

JENNI: Yeah, Hillsborough wouldn't have happened had he been there on the day.

SHEILA: *(Returning to her seat and speaking directly to the audience.)* A lot of people would say it was a disaster waiting to happen!

FRIEND: Certain officers at South Yorkshire were a bit miffed about this and when a new man came in to take charge, they gave him very little co-operation. This new man, Duckenfield, was university educated not a hairy arse copper. Mole was a hairy arse copper's copper, this new guy was totally different...and they wanted him to make a mess at the first available opportunity. The first big job he had to do was Hillsborough so he got no co-operation from his men whatsoever...they wanted

him to fuck up, sorry excuse, they wanted him to
make a mess…er they didn't want 96 to die, but
they wanted him to make a mess and er…and he
did.

JENNI: Yeah and that's why I always blame Murray,
he's the main culprit in all of this, he's dead now,
he's out of the picture – Murray was Mole's best
mate.

FRIEND: Yeah he should have nursed Duckenfield
through it.

JENNI: For me Hillsborough was quite simple, you
know, somebody opened the gate and let people
into already overcrowded pens, they were being
crushed to death from half-past two, quarter to three
onwards. I have evidence on that, on my daughters
own evidence, so I've known that all this time.
They said they couldn't see that – so the police lied
about that, they got rid of the tape that showed how
overcrowded the pens were. *(Pause.)* And Taylor
came to the conclusion that the opening of those
gates was a mistake at the highest magnitude – not
mistake, it was a blunder of the highest magnitude.
Now that wasn't allowed to be used in the inquest.
You couldn't hear evidence after 3.15.

ANNE WILLIAMS: The coroner decided to put a 3.15
cut-off point, the reason he argued was that the
victims would have been dead or brain dead by that
time. No evidence was heard after that time. I have
tracked down 5 people who have helped my son
Kevin after 3.15 that day, 3 Liverpool fans, an off-
duty police officer and a PC who was on duty at the
time. The two fans, Stevie Hart and Tony O'Keefe,
pulled Kevin out of the pens at 3.28, they carried
him to the North Stand. Both say that Kevin was
alive. They left Kevin with a police officer who said
he would look after him. The police officer then

walked away! Johnny Prescott another Liverpool
fan came across Kevin, saw he was alive and ran to
get help. In the meantime, an off-duty police officer,
Derek Bruder had seen Kevin lying in front of a
police cordon moving his head and left his seat to
help him. Not one police officer would break the
cordon to help him. When Mr Bruder got to Kevin,
Johnny Prescott was with him and the St John's
Ambulance man. They carried out resuscitation and
heart massage, Mr Bruder found a pulse and at 3.37
(Beat.) an ambulance came on to the pitch going
towards the Leppings Lane end of the ground.
Mr Bruder shouted for someone to stop it – the
ambulance wouldn't stop. Johnny Prescott stayed
with Kevin when PC Martin came to take Kevin
to the gym. Johnny helped put Kevin on a trolley,
Miss Martin was told to stay and carry out heart
massage and resuscitation. She put Kevin in the
part of the gym that was set aside for the injured…
She found a pulse and after resuscitation Kevin's
ribs started to move so thinking she had him alive,
she picked Kevin up in her arms. It was then that
Kevin opened his eyes, murmured the word 'mum',
slumped back and died in her arms at 4.00pm.

JENNI: – I don't think it's a coincidence, it must be his
Peter Wright's style of policing mustn't it? Because
he went in very hard on the miners and he went in
very hard in Toxteth with CS gas. My God…y'know
I didn't realise *(Cough.)* what a history he had. Why
has it taken so long? Well this is what has made
me think that it had to be a water tight conspiracy,
a cover-up or whatever else you want to call it,
anything not water tight would have gotten through
before. Margaret Thatcher was quite a tough
woman when you think about it. *(Pause.)* It had to
come from the top! I do think it was a conspiracy
between the government, the hierarchy and the
police.

ANNE: Evidence has been suppressed, statements have been changed, there has never been a full inquiry into how Kevin died. Three times my appeal was submitted, three times it was refused – no one wants to answer for the mistakes that were made after 3.15.

ROB: I think the 3.15 cut off is a deliberate attempt to not allow information out into the public domain as it would have had to have been heard in court, 'What happened after 3.15? Why didn't you make use of the ambulance crew?' But because of the cut off as soon as somebody in the inquiry started to mention something, 'oh yeah I saw...' hang on what time was that, 3.18? Sorry!' Not gonna listen!

STEPHEN: Why has no one answered what happened to the CCTV tapes? The police tapes, they went missing straight after Hillsborough – funny that!

ROB WHITE: Erm...I've spoken to Trevor Hicks *(Looks across at JENNY.)* about this and he's pretty confident that there was a video tape from the police control office which would have shown what happened and that somehow went missing the day after Hillsborough, seems very suspicious doesn't it, erm because that would have been extremely helpful in a court of law and in dispelling a lot of the stories that came out. *(Pause.)*

FRIEND: The thing to remember is, the thing that scandalises me is what's the purpose of the police force if it isn't to protect, er to protect people and establish truth...you know that's – that's why they exist...and so this notion of the copper changing his statement because he's been advised to by this lawyer negates his very existence, there's a lot more of that to come out isn't there...I think Jen

JENNI: oh yeah

FRIEND: the extent of the changed statements it's just –

JENNI: and the conspiracy

FRIEND: yep…a copper –

JENNI: between the government

FRIEND: oh yeah, yeah

JENNI: the police, the press…I think that's the major thing that's got to come out from this release of documents, that there was a conspiracy…I just hope that there's evidence to back that up…cos you couldn't just get a few coppers fiddling the books and it being this watertight. And the knock on effect because he hasn't told the truth and the effect it's had on the families' lives…because the truth wasn't told…and it's left us still twenty-three years down the line still looking for truth.

SHEILA: Allegedly according to Andy Hymas, the senior police officer on the day, he says that Assistant Chief Walter Jackson was cowering under his desk.

STEPHEN KELLY: Do you know not long after Hillsborough the police turned up at me house? I look out of the window and there's two cars, South Yorkshire Police and West Midlands police, they were the investigating force for all inquiries into Hillsborough. They had both turned up at the same time. I had West Midlands in the front room and South Yorkshire in the back. South Yorks had a bag of stuff that they thought was our Mike's. Mike had lost a shoe and his jacket, he had a pair of Hi-Tec trainers on, grey Hi-Tec, they were horrible. So the police had this big plastic bag and they kept bringing out stuff – Nikes, Tachinis – they brought out another pair and I says again, 'I told you his were crap, Mike would never have worn them', and they threw a big plastic bag on our table – our dining table, it flew open and it was a black coat covered in vomit. 'I told you he had a blue coat,' I says, 'don't yous ever learn? Wrong trainees, wrong coat – how can I ever eat off that table again without thinking what happened to that lad? When will yous ever learn?' *(Pause.)* As soon as the police left, me wife said 'get rid of the table' – then the house and then we drifted apart.

ROB: One of the things that still sticks with all of us who were there on that day is that within fifteen, twenty minutes of it happening so at about twenty-past three – representatives from the FA went to the Police Commander and asked 'What's happened?' He said that fans have forced down the gates. That was the chief police officer that was in charge that day and he would have known that that comment would have gone beyond the FA representative and within a few minutes of that, the message had gone out to the press around the world

(Long pause whilst ROB composes himself. Voice trembling.) …an…and 23 years later people still remember that first message more than they remember any other message and that's why people like us find it very difficult when you're talking about justice to think there's lots that's been said after that but basically it was a deliberate attempt to shift the blame it started at that point and what subsequently followed all flowed from that decision at that point. It was then a case of well we can't kind of put that back in the bottle now so we've just gotta go with this and that's the thing that really gets us the most that we know that that is untrue.

FRIEND: Yeah…yeah…there's an old expression isn't there er…'a lie is half way round the world before truth gets its boots on'… I think that's a really good expression

JENNI: yeah I do

STEPHEN: It's not right, and it's about time somebody had the guts to stand up and say 'y'know, it wasn't the supporters' fault it was ours.' Give them broken people some relief y'know. Give the city some repair. Cos realistically most of the guys that were at the match are all knocking 60 now and so it's, it's… it's hard, harder to deal with when your older, cos y'know, I've seen all my family go – our Mike, me ma, me sister Joan and my son – and I'm thinking please god. Meself last year I had a heart thing and I'm thinking please god let me see the justice and go and tell my family, even it's only by their graves y'know.

STEVE clearly upset gets up and goes to stand next to KENNY, he reacts strongly to the next few lines.

FRIEND: I want the Sun boycott to go on and on and I want – I want things to be revealed and I want the Hillsborough families to sue the arses off them…to sue them for millions and millions

STEVE: *(In anger overlapping.)* It's not about the money!

FRIEND: because the only way public sssssssssss-safety improves is if it costs money…if accidents cost money, cos it's cost effective in this country to take risks for public safety.

SHEILA: *(Aside.)* Isn't funny that the ones who go on about money are the ones with money?

FRIEND: You're b-b-bound to go and see rock bands play, they're death traps they just pile – you're often on a slope like – there's thousands of yous, you're trying to get near the front, there's people coming and going…you know they're death traps…it costs them nothing to do that…, you know the worst thing to happen is a plane of lawyers, if a plane full of lawyers crashes it's a catastrophe, you know that's expensive…they've got wives and kids and big expensive wages, the compensation is huge…and when young people die…nothing!

JENNI: Oh yeah well we were more or less told anyone who was over eighteen without any dependents, like Sarah who was at university, it was actually saving Trevor and I money by her dying because we didn't have to pay her university fees, her hall fees and all of this stuff…so Sarah's life actually wasn't worth anything. They don't have to pay anything to parents losing teenagers…and at the time because Vicky was under eighteen ermmm, the value of Victoria's life was £3500 pounds

FRIEND: it's cost effective – …it's amazing isn't it… amazing

JENNI: We saved money by losing Sarah!

FRIEND: yeah…hence they don't care about safety because it doesn't cost them nothing…they must measure the risk against the cost, the cost of removing the –

JENNI: They will do

ROB: There have been a series of disasters in the 1980s around Zeebrugge, King's Cross and it was just kind of a culture in Britain that you know, sloppy, sloppy health and safety. Once you'd gone through those gates there was no turning back, you couldn't go against the flow of people coming behind you, so even at half-past two we were kind of penned in, and it wasn't until you got through that you could see really how bad it was; people were being forced up against the walls between the turnstiles, forced into the side walls, forced into that concertina gate, and really that situation itself was dangerous, I mean there were people crying out, 'there's people dying down here.' The police were just letting more and more people through, and so you can picture it, you've got a build-up of people behind you, you can't move forward, you can't move back. They were just screaming at supporters to move away from the front, well you can't do that when you're forced up against the wall. They needed to direct people behind you, but there seemed to be a sort of complete lack of control, people were swaying from side to side and it was chaotic, erm and because of that build-up and the danger that existed there the police were presented with a decision as to what they had to do to try and alleviate that problem because if it had been allowed to continue then I'm pretty sure that people would have died out there, up until that point that was the worst crush I'd ever experienced. So I'm not surprised that the police took the decision to open the gate to allow fans to get out of that awful situation so I don't condemn what they did. But where they made, and what's described in The Taylor Report as, a monumental blunder, is they didn't do anything about the consequence of opening that gate.

FRIEND: So therefore whenever anything happens sue the arse...you know make it the most expensive disaster in British legal history...at the moment it's been the cheapest. Fourteen – fourteen South Yorkshire coppers who policed Hillsborough, a few years after Hillsborough er – er alleged that they had post traumatic distress disorder, PTSD, they sued their employer and fourteen South Yorkshire coppers walked away between them with one point two million pounds...the families of the dead and the dead didn't get anywhere near that sum erm in other words...

SHEILA: They didn't want money

FRIEND: and the main ingredient of PTSD is guilt, any psychologist will tell you that, you know guilt of the survivor etcetera...in other words for the guilt, you

know for their guilt in killing you know all those
people, they got more than the people they killed…
than the families of the people killed

JENNI: And not a lot of people know that the disaster
fund that was set up erm wasn't just for the
families…the bereaved families…anybody who
was in that ground that day, including all South
Yorkshire police officers, anybody who was in that
ground that day could claim from the fund. Not that
it's about money –

SHEILA: You're right, it's not about money…but the
reality is, it was in the 80s when there was high
unemployment, so many of those who died were
in that young age group, but also so many of the
survivors were of an age, you know, whereby it's
not nice saying, 'you're not worth much', but aside
from that, those that did take cases, most of their
cases were settled for very small amounts of money
say 800/1100 pounds. Now we know that to treat
someone for post-traumatic stress disorder costs
thousands, we know what we pay out in helping
survivors from HJC. What happens was, and this
is where solicitors can be seen as sharks in suits,
not always, there are good legal people. But erm,
there was a lot of 'ambulance chasing' that went on
before that term was popular. But people signed up
to be with specific firms and specific solicitor's firms
stood out, and it came to our attention that most
people had settled cases and what had happened
was, we found out was, just before Christmas, the
first Christmas after Hillsborough, so many of these
fellas were unemployed, they had young families.
They'd get a solicitor's phone call, 'Look you can
settle your case for 800 pound, you can settle you
case for 1100 pound.' That's the kids' Christmas
presents and food on the table, so they took it.
(Phone rings.) Sorry. *(Answers phone.)*

Sorry I'm in a meeting at the moment, can I call you back?

STEPHEN: I've never had compensation, I've never asked for compensation and I will never accept compensation. All of us work for this campaign voluntary, y'know a million hours here and there, but y'know that's it. I'd do a million more if it takes it – to get the truth.

JENNI: It's about accountability…cos there are so many myths about Hillsborough aren't there

FRIEND: I'm only talking about money cos I think- I think it's w-what you do is you pass on your gain to the next generation…and by making it expensive that's a gain because your safety will be improved –

JENNI: Oh that's the only way you're going to improve the safety…erm but there you go

STEPHEN: I've spent a third of my life chasing this. It cost me sister her life, our Joan was a bit of a mess – she was going at it too much, going to Leeds, Sheffield, London. Chasing this, chasing that – it started to affect her health. Then Mum died – Joan's going at it too much and I said look we've got to stop it, she said, 'me brother's dead' and I said 'yeah but you've got one who's living'. I regret saying that – when she died, I took up the mantle more, not to let Joan and Michael down. It consumes you. I don't know if I've got the strength to carry on.

SHEILA: People can't move on because they feel they are letting down the dead. It's impacted on their lives in so many ways. Marriages have broken down and relationships have broken down, children have gone off the rails, you know, the brothers and sisters of the deceased. People aren't vengeful and it's so sad that the cover-up is such that people are forced to react whereby they might appear aggressive, they might appear spiteful. But these aren't the real people, it's the way things are thrust at them that they have to react and respond.

NEIL: I've lived with a lot of guilt about that day…but you know at the time you try and bury these things. Which is the worst possible thing I could have done. Because when you try and bury such deep-seated psychological events they tend to resurface in the future which is exactly what happened with me. About 10 years ago I started to suffer from anxiety for no apparent reason…all of a sudden I get those same feelings that I had in that crush…

ROB WHITE: I was standing next to a girl erm…who basically was pressed up against my arm, she was having real difficulty breathing erm…and she was sort of, her head was looking at me like this *(Turns head.)* and she couldn't speak, she was in so much pain, her head was here and there was another body that sort of had her head in a vice with my arm and…what she did…when I looked at her she started tapping on my foot with her own foot, and erm, started vigorously tapping so I knew she was trying to say something sort of, her tear-filled eyes were just staring at me, pleading, 'help me, help me'. So I called out to a police woman on the other side of the fence erm…and she looked at me – so I know she heard me – I said 'look this, this girl's in desperate need of help can you please try and reach over and grab her?' and she looked at me and she just looked away. And sadly the girl did die but there was absolutely nothing I could do, or anybody else could do for her, she died whilst she was standing next to me and I, you know I was stood like this, unable to move, nobody else could move we just saw her die. And that does something to you.

Silence – ROB takes a drink of water.

KENNY: I still feel guilty now 23 years on. When you think about that person who stood in front of you, how did they get on? Is he alright? The person who pulled me up into the stands – what's he doing with his life? Is he alright?

ROB: It's really hard as a survivor er when everybody's sort of saying to ya, it's great to see you and sorry you've been through that but you know time's a great healer that's what everybody used to say *(Long pause.)* you know it's 23 years since that happened and you can see that it still affects me now erm and it will, it will always affect me.

Silence.

SHEILA: What I was going to say about the panel…

JENNI: We trust the people in the panel.

SHEILA: The panel – It's something that wouldn't have been there only for this group fighting. The Family Support Group say that they have every faith in the panel. The HJC cannot have the same trust as we do not have the same relationship with the panel. It has been clear that the HFSG have a more intimate relationship with the panel members.

JENNI: It's not about the HJC or the HFSG – the documents will be released to all family members before the public, before the supporters and survivors because they have to.

STEPHEN: *(To the audience.)* Following the release of the papers by the government – the panel are gonna come up with this erm…what they call an archive of what happened at Hillsborough. It's not an inquest.

JENNI: We trust the Bishop of Liverpool, he's on the panel.

SHEILA: The last meeting Barry Devonshire had with Bishop James, him and his wife asked for a private meeting and when they got there they were expecting to just be the two of them and then three officers from the Home Office came walking in – Barry wanted to know certain things about his son Christopher who'd died and in the middle of the meeting he tells Barry that Christopher had some skin taken from him and that he could have been one of ten of the victims who'd had post-mortems that they now couldn't recognise whose skin it was to which body! And as I said to him when he rang me that night – how did the Bishop of Liverpool know that their son had skin taken from him before his parents did?

I think it's important to remember that this is an indication of the insensitivity families have had to deal with. The coroner walked into the court one day, and because the inquest went on and on and on he announced 'ooh erm special day today we're eligible for the Guiness Book of Records for the longest inquest for British legal history'! That'll be in the transcripts, that was the level we're dealing with!

WENDY enters carrying shopping bags.

JENNI: *(Determined.)* You know we as a subcommittee from the Family Support Group have dealt with the subcommittee from the panel. There's some very good people with a lot of expertise in various fields, ermm…you know data protection – there's an expert in that, everything really, there's a lawyer on there. They know the history of Hillsborough and will know if something isn't right, or if something is missing. Well, the subcommittee will probably see the stuff first, then the families and erm…it'll well it's going to be released to the public in September, one of the worst things that could happen to the families is to see bits of it coming out bit by bit erm, you know in the media. It's just the volume of the documents… We'd rather they delayed erm and look at them thoroughly, even if it takes until next year. That's better than missing something.

STEPHEN: The panel won't name names, they won't lay blame on any door. And as I said…there's 96 families to appease – siblings, aunts, uncles…a lot of people… And from my belief of what the panel are gonna come up with, it won't end…sadly… because I might get some information released about Michael an' I could be happy with that but another family won't. And I'm the only member of my family left, so I'm a bit of an easy target aren't I but where there's five, six brothers an' sisters…it's gonna cause friction with the other families…which it has over the years.

JENNI: It's taken 23 years to get to this turning point – and of course legally they don't have to release it anyway, cos there's a 30-year rule isn't there?

SHEILA: You should never be grateful for crumbs.

FRIEND: I'm sorry Jen', I've gotta go.

JENNI: Alright, yeah, bye.

He exits.

NEIL: It is criminal that it's taken so long to get to this position…those who would have been held accountable, they're all retired, moved to a different job or died…

STEPHEN: Our lines of communication with the panel are terrible… I've challenged the Bishop about this…I think there's gonna be a massive fall out because we are gonna find out things that we really don't wanna know. So it's gonna be very traumatic – there's gonna be more people suffering depressions, needing psychiatric services and no systems in place.

JENNI: Oh…god no…there will be support systems in place – even after the drama, Granada TV set up helplines and they got calls all night. There's got to be because it's huge…

SHEILA: *(Interrupting JENNI.)* I know about the helplines, I was on one of the phone lines on my 40th birthday on that night.

NEIL: I can see that a lot of hurt may come for a lot of people when the truth comes out. I can see that for those who think it's such a long time ago now and they've had all the hurt and they've learnt to cope with it, it's opening old wounds and for a lot of people that could be unbearable. So I can see an argument against releasing the papers…

STEPHEN: It's not only families…I mean last February there was this young man Steven Bignall who was at the game, erm he suffered in silence all this time and I say, last February unfortunately decided to put himself in front of a train. Now he's another victim of Hillsborough.

NEIL: When you think about the effect that it's had on people's lives, when I was having counselling and I was thinking well there's people who've died… people who've lost their erm sons, daughters, brothers, sisters, mothers, fathers whatever…so I never sought out any help as there were always other people who needed that help more than me.

NEIL exits.

Beat.

WENDY: The group helped me in life generally when my [first] husband died I felt like I've got people to rely on yanno I can ring them and talk and erm when I came up here the season after, it was very hard yanno but I did feel I got support there from the group *(Chuckles.)*

STEVE ROTHERHAM MP walks in – looks at seated cast and indicates the groups.

STEVE ROTHERHAM: So you've got the Hillsborough Family Support Group *(JENNI exits.)*, the Hillsborough Justice Campaign *(SHEILA exits.)* and now Hope for Hillsborough *(ANNE exits.)* – It's like 'The Life of Brian', with The People's Front of Judea and The Judean People's Front – they all basically want the same thing but wanna go about it very differently and it's very sad...

STEPHEN: *(Looks at STEVE ROTHERHAM then directly to audience.)* If we'd have stayed together we might have won this now.

STEPHEN KELLY exits. KENNY and WENDY come DS.

KENNY: And we ended up getting married. Been married two years now on Tuesd...Monday innit.

WENDY: Yeh *(They both laugh.)*

KENNY: Me wedding was the best day of me life.

WENDY: Sheila kept saying it's our first wedding.

KENNY: Our first Hillsborough wedding!

Taxi Scene

*Actor, ROGAN TAYLOR walks on C.S. Projection: Liverpool streets –
Anfield. Places his two chairs down next to each other. As scene progresses
projection takes us through the Liverpool streets.*

*Two other actors enter S.L and S.R. Each have two chairs with them.
They place them down, facing the audience.*

ACTOR: Rogan Taylor, writer, broadcaster and Director
of the Football Industry Group.

ACTOR: Steve Rotherham, Labour MP, Liverpool.

ACTOR: Brian Reade, Sports journalist for *The Daily
Mirror.*

ALL: Taxi!

*Three actors playing taxi drivers enter, each carrying a chair and they
each place in front of the others. The action takes up the whole stage.*

ROGAN: You know when somebody first paid me to
think about football, pretty neat eh? *(Pause.)* Erm, I
wrote down FOOT, BALL and FAN. *(Pause.)* And
I spent a couple of months unpacking that *(Pause.)*
because there's something absolutely weird about
football. What does the word 'fan' mean? Yeah…
it's short for fanatic. Outside of Palestine and one
or two other odd places in the world – fanaticism
is not something that attracts ordinary people is it?
You've kinda got to give your life away. You know
who wants to be a fanatic? You know what Italians
call football fans? It's Tifosi, T.I.F.O.S.I. – what
does it mean, exactly what it says – 'tifosi', people
with typhus. The Tifosi – anyone fancy typhus?
Actually no – I'll give it a miss if you don't mind.
In Brazil – the word is torcedor, T.O.R.C.E.D.O.R,
it comes from the verb, to wring water out of
washing – the English would be, 'the mangled

one!'. Anyone wanna get mangled? No, I think I'll give that a miss as well. So the words that fans used for being a fan describe a condition that no sane human being would actually volunteer for, isn't that weird? So on 15 April 1989 – I'm at Hillsborough, not in Leppings Lane but in the West Stand and we watched the disaster unfold.

STEVE ROTHERHAM: I was there, but I swapped my ticket, 15 minutes, it was probably even less than that before the start of the game. I'd gone there the year before, semi-final against Nottingham Forest, very differently policed but uncomfortable in those pens, I was a brickie then, not a politician – so I was fit, not like now *(Laughs.)* and I was feeling the pressure, and so this year, even though I had one for the Leppings Lane end I thought, I'll try and swap this. I tried for a bit and eventually someone said, 'here are, I'll have that an' go with me mates'. So I didn't know this lad but we swapped and they went in…and so that always plays on ya mind a little bit.

TAXI DRIVER 1: Cos I remember when I first 'eard the news it had been delayed, I was made up cos it meant I'd get home in time to watch the match… you know, before I realised what was 'appening. I 'ad mates there yeah, they were a little bit older than me though about 15, 16… They don't even talk about it *(All drivers switch to right arm on wheel.)* Me mates, they got, they got squashed, they were in the crush, never talk about it cos they were petrified, absolutely petrified.

BRIAN READE: Back in the 1980s football fans were basically treated as a problem. That's why, at Hillsborough, fans were in cages, why, when they called out for help the police ignored them, and why when the dying spilled out onto the pitch, instead of trying to save lives the police formed a line across the centre of the pitch, with dogs, believing rival fans were about to riot.

TAXI DRIVER 2: Don't forget, Liverpool was a hated city back then. So it was like anything they could get on them it was like… *(Punching out fists.)* Bang, bang, bang, bang, bang.

ROGAN: Regardless of what you think, what would you say were the attributes of Scousers? What's Scouserdom? I mean there are many commonalities between other cities where you've got large, what we would call working-class populations, heavy drinking, whole bunch of stuff that goes with it, crime…

TAXI DRIVER 1: Yanno, when Liverpool, in like the 70s and 80s – were always in Europe, well all the criminals from all over the country – not just Liverpool would travel with them cos it's an excuse to get out of the country. Say Liverpool were playin' in Sweden…or Switzerland, then all the robbers from all over the country would go wit' them and try and rob all the boss shops – but cos it was the Liverpool team there, they'd get the reputation. And it weren't just people from Liverpool – don't get me wrong some of 'em did, but not just Liverpool.

ROGAN: This is many moons ago – a couple of decades at least. Princess Margaret was arriving at Everton Brow to open a new Sports Centre and I just happened to be in the news room when the news broke, the Princess' limo sort of turned the corner and was driving up to the front of this new place and erm the red carpet had been rolled out, and you know in between the car coming into sight and the red carpet going down…someone nicked the red carpet. When we heard that we just fell about laughin' because it was like the ultimate Scouse crime, it was committed against the upper class. It was cheeky, meaningless. What do you do with 50 yards of red carpet?

BRIAN READE: The Establishment have thwarted efforts to get to the truth at every step of the way because they know there was an organised cover-up which went right to the top.

STEVE ROTHERHAM: I tried to dispel the myths in my speech in the House of Commons, I tried to pull apart the idea of ticketless fans or drunken hooligans and you know it's interesting isn't it when Jeremy Hunt…

TAXI DRIVER 1: Cunt…I know why the interviewer said that now.

STEVE ROTHERHAM: …hmm. Who has now got himself into trouble for something completely different, but when he made reference to hooliganism he mentioned Hillsborough, and it shows ya that yanno two and a half decades on there are still people, senior politicians not havin' the intelligence to check the independence of those accounts from all those years ago.

ROGAN: Why was the system worked the way it was?…There's something very English about this. There's a couple of disasters you may not of heard of… Heysel – didn't happen in England – it was Belgium, what happened after Heysel well the chairman of the FA got six months in jail. Hillsborough, 96 people dead, the match commander, David Duckenfield, who lies directly within five minutes saying the fans knocked the doors down – when he in fact opened them and it's er…'not me gov'…hahaha you know typical grim reaction, what happened to Duckenfield? Nothin', retired on full pension, what happened to the English FA? Whose match it was – nothin'. Isn't it odd?

BRIAN READE: I hope that when the papers are released, a complete and truthful picture of the day's events, plus the causes and the aftermath, can be established. I hope that shows, what I have always believed as someone who was there, that Liverpool fans have been terribly maligned for their behaviour and that the bereaved families have been deliberately lied to. And I hope, at the very least, that the Prime Minister stands up in the House of Commons and issues a long and sincere apology to everyone affected.

TAXI DRIVER 3: You've got as much chance of that 'appenin' as Alan Davies getting a gig at the Empire. I used to like him, thought he was funny, if I saw him now I'd...

BRIAN READE: If I saw him, I'd say, 'I never took you for such a self-pitying fool'.

TAXI DRIVER 2: Tell you another one I hate – that Kelvin MacKenzie – what he said in *The Sun*, it was lies, we know it was lies. Apparently he phones up Kenny, Kenny Dalglish and says, 'Kenny, it's Kelvin, how can I put it right?' And Kenny says, 'Get *The Sun* to put the headline, 'The Truth, We lied'. He didn't do it. So we don't buy *The Sun* – scum. It was just to sell papers, and they knew back then, there'd be no aftermath, the papers could say what they wanted.

STEVE ROTHERHAM: I won't swear, but did you see *Question Time?* That despicable person, MacKenzie was on, a man who dehumanised a human tragedy. I think it's important that we put him under as much scrutiny as he forced our city and the people of Liverpool and certainly the victims, survivors and families of Hillsborough – as much as he put them under. I'd love to get yanno film crew and press packs yanno all around his house on a daily basis because that's what happened to the likes of the Hicks'.

ROGAN: *The Sun* headlines, it's still not over is it. And what we, yah know the headlines every day from the Leveson inquiry, is just constant re-affirmation of what the Scousers knew 20 years ago, that these bastards don't care about anybody. If the South Yorkshire Police want this story told and Mrs T wants to do the South Yorkshire Police a favour because they biffed up the unions, sure, we'll have a headline – 'The Truth – they pissed on their own people,' why not? That's who we're dealing with here, the people who tapped Millie Dowler's phone, the people who deleted her messages off her phone to her parents.

STEVE ROTHERHAM: 23 years ago, the people of Merseyside took the bold decision to say that they thought there was some collusion between senior members of the government, police officers and the press, an' 23 years ago, everyone was goin', 'don't be ridiculous.' I'm on the DCMS committee an' believe me we were right, there's not even a miniscule of percentage of me that thinks we weren't right in what we thought.

TAXI DRIVER 3: This bugger reckons he's gonna cut in front of me…no chance mate.

STEVE ROTHERHAM: I agonised literally over every word in the speech that I made and decided at the last minute to read the names out. The only person I'd ran it through to was Sandra, me wife and I couldn't get to the names because I erm kept filling up. Nobody had ever read out names of any victims before, the only time that ever happens is when the Prime Minister reads out on a Wednesday before PMQs the names of any fallen from Afghanistan or Iraq, so I was very conscious that I didn't want the people in Parliament to be pissed off thinking 'who does he think he is?' I didn't want them to think I'm a bouncy Scouser, I am a bouncy Scouser but I didn't want them to think that. On the other hand I knew the importance that perhaps when you hear their names and their ages that it might get over to these very tough politicians sittin' round the chamber the enormity of the loss, yanno when I did John Paul, an he was ten, I think I was trying to concentrate on what I was saying but there was an audible 'dear me' when I said ten years of age and they took his blood alcohol levels in case he was drunk and so I think those kind of things hit home.

ROGAN: You know to outsiders Liverpool looks like the kind of place where all the spears point outwards and if you mess with them then they'll never forget it. But when you get in the city you realise that they're stabbing each other which is why we've never had a local government worthy of its name. It's weird – a weird mix with a strange solidarity. You know the first scarf on the Shankley gates after Hillsborough wasn't a red one, it was blue.

TAXI DRIVER 1: Here you go Lime Street…nice talking to you. *(Projection off.)*

STEVE ROTHERHAM: *(Exits taxi.)* You know Cameron, he's just like Thatcher…only **he** wears more make-up.

KENNY and WENDY enter, they arrange three chairs DS for final scene.

KENNY: [We] got married at 12 o'clock, high noon wasn't it?

WENDY: Yeah yeah.

KENNY: What was the wedding songs we had? I can't, can't, 'I can't help falling in love with you', wasn't it?

WENDY: Yeah, yeah.

KENNY: 'I wanna hold your hand'.

WENDY: Yeah.

KENNY: And what was the other one?

WENDY: It must be love.

KENNY: Must be love.

WENDY: We were trying to pick all this romantic classical stuff that neither of us really knew anything about

KENNY: about

WENDY: So we thought oh sod that we'll just have some modern things yanno *(Chuckles.)*

KENNY: In the night time it was err Frankie Goes to Hollywood, 'The Power of Love'

WENDY: yeah.

KENNY: Had that on, our dance song.

(They exit holding hands.)

Act Three – Waiting

STEPHEN KELLY, JENNI HICKS and SHEILA COLEMAN stand at the side of the chairs looking directly at the audience.

STEPHEN/JENNI/SHEILA: Waiting.

They sit. Beat.

SHEILA: People say to me, 'well what do you think justice is?', 'When do you think is a good time?'. Er, 'what do you think? When will families say that's enough?' *(Beat.)* And what I always say is what I think it would be, it might be different to where other people will think it will be. Where I think, for me, it would be if there was a ruling. Somewhere along the lines of you know, like the ruling that came out of the Bloody Sunday tribunal after all those years, you would never have thought that following on from 1972, that a Tory Prime Minister would stand up in the House of Commons and say sorry to Irish people and for the families of those who were murdered, erm that was just so beyond the realms of anything. If there was a formal ruling, that said there was an injustice, lies were told, there was a cover-up.

JENNI: I've learnt so much in the last 23 years about people, I look back and I thought I was quite a woman of the world then but my god, the way things really work, the political aspect, the cover-ups, I mean we were just Mr and Mrs Joe Bloggs getting on with our lives like everyone else.

STEPHEN: Ahh, err, I suppose the biggest word I can say is frustration. Yaknow, you always seem to hear something in the news an' you think there's a bit of light at the end of the tunnel, but it always seems to be overturned, or dragged on again. You feel as though you got over one hurdle only to find another one. It's heartbreaking really because you er, you want it to end. Yaknow we've... I've wanted this to end for, as I say for 23 years, and I wish to God it would. I can't move on till I find out why? Our Mike's not dead, he's still here in limbo, they won't allow him to rest and for a Roman Catholic that's not good.

SHEILA: Erm...because...there's an issue around people saying they'll never give up, and I don't buy into that, but I do think those people deserve a life, those Hillsborough families, whatever's left of their lives they deserve to be able to live them, knowing they've done, as much as they can. I've seen people walk away, so disillusioned by the system, someone who used to be chair of our group actually, a bereaved father, who saw his wife die, and he had cancer, and he just went, whatever's left of my life I'm just going to live it, I'm never going to get justice from the corrupt society, so he just lived out his life with a sense of sneering really at the system. Because...the facts will emerge, no two ways about it, erm very valuable facts, erm, but what will happen with those facts I don't know.

STEPHEN: The other day was an example. When I was driving and they was just playing a Beatles song, and I was made up, bit of a sunny day, there in the Pool, driving along and I'd just come from speaking to the students at John Moores Uni, I was in a happy mood you know, fine, not a problem and then the radio, one o'clock news. It just said, 'breaking news...er...Hills...' and you just hear the word Hillsborough and you go on a down, you do. I had to pull over, stop, compose meself an' then you start welling up straight away. You just... and you know there's no rhyme or reason why, it just does. Yaknows, as soon as you hear that word Hillsborough, it knocks you sideways.

JENNI: I DO think it's time now to find some kind of peace with it, not just for the families erm, obviously families have to find an individual…whatever it is with them, no matter what word you use to some families it's not the right one. Errrrm…it's either peace, or closure or whatever, because for the families there will never be total closure on it because f-for me, my children…you know, I'm no longer a mum, I don't have children anymore so that is a very different thing to the public ermm… yanno to the public injustice aswell. But I do think Liverpool and the city needs to find some kind of closure with it as well. I do

SHEILA: But like, for some people, erm, there are obsessive elements, there are people who are obsessed. *(Pause.)* But I do think this is where I have an advantage over say families or survivors in that as much as I erm, I can stand back, I didn't lose anyone, and maybe they do want it to go on forever, but I actually don't think that's healthy for them either.

STEPHEN: It's cos it's dragged so much out of you as a person over the years. I mean, as I said this has been a third of my life. I'm 59. *(Beat.)* Twenty-three years I've been challenging and struggling against this. And you know, for something I never done, something Michael never done and something the other lads and girls never done.

SHEILA: John Glover, John had three sons who went to Hillsborough – only two came back. The other one is dead and one remains traumatized. John is dying why couldn't he have had the reports yanno?

STEPHEN: If someone could say to me, erm. 'it wasn't the fans' fault, the-the-the police lost control that day, which has undoubtedly been proven, the papers lied and then, 'we apologise to the families' why that's me. I don't want more than that and that you know I can then say, cos, cos one of my last converstations with me mum before she died was, err…was *(Voice weaker, holding back tears.)* she said, 'was Mike a hooligan?' *(Wells up, quietly.)* Sorry…she died thinking he was a hooligan. *(Fights back tears again.)* Sorry… *(Composes himself and says strongly.)* And he wasn't!

SHEILA: I wish you'd met John, you'd like him – proper Scouse. You should see his wife Theresa and his daughter Luli – they're still fighting.

JENNI: I do believe that if it had happened in another city I think this would have died a death a long time ago and the injustice of what happened on that day, they would have been more likely to have gotten away with it. But the people of this city won't allow that. And I know that some people will say, oh it's time to put it away now, and we've got friends who are not involved and they'll say, you need to move on now and they've been telling you that for years but you can't when you know it's such a huge injustice, you know you have to make it right.

SHEILA: There's times when I go, erm so a few years ago, round the time of the 20th anniversary, I went, I'm moving on, I'll be honest, we all have battle fatigue, you know, and I'm no saint, I'm not superwoman, erm and er, I went you know, 'I will take it to this stage, and then other people have got to do it', it should always be that way anyway, there should always be new blood coming in. And erm that was when Andy Burnham turned up and everyone was shouting 'justice', and before I knew it I was just immersed in it all again, but I still think erm I have had to reassess, I used to say, I will walk away when there's an achievement. And I've also had to realise that, I, I have real problems dealing with failure, erm, I take it really badly. It takes guts to know when, there's no shame in it, I learnt that as an adult of middle age to accept failure, but there was no shame in it, in fact it was an indication of how we fought, you know and so what I'm saying is, anything beyond things with the Justice Campaign, I wouldn't want to play a hands-on role.

STEPHEN: For me…you've got the Justice Campaign, the Family Support Group and now Hope for Hillsborough, we should be walking 96 of us hand in hand – I would give anything to see that.

JENNI: Basically for me, I'm just waiting for this new evidence to come out to see if there's anything that I've missed. I actually think that it's going to be worse than I think. What I would like is for them to change the verdict of accidental death – if the evidence is all there, then that is not a lawful verdict, it was achieved by the evidence being doctored, by the myths and lies at the time, so I'm hoping they'll change the inquest verdict to unlawfully killed.

Beat.

Even if it does come out and nothing happens, I mean lots of things are out of time now anyway, we're not naive with that, we are aware of that, we do know that, I think for the truth to be out there is the most important thing. I'm hoping that it'll open a lot of eyes.

SHEILA: Some of us have a theory, part of the reason they want to delay the release of the papers is that they are waiting for Thatcher to die. And at the end of the day, she is someone's mother and you respect the dying and the dead. But – there is no love lost on Merseyside for Margaret Thatcher and what she did to the city. There's a school of thought which says Hillsborough was payback time for Thatcher, she allowed the cover-up, this was her way of thanking the South Yorkshire Police for the help they gave her in breaking the miners in the 80s. Right away when the government appealed and this is what I love about Liverpool fans and how quick they are, right away someone made a banner saying, 'Expose the Lies before Thatcher dies!'. These families weren't political extremists that want to smash the state or whatever. These were people whose kids had gone to a football match and didn't come home.

JENNI: Well, I've done my best and erm to achieve that, it's taken a long time. However, erm…if it-it-it's not gonna bring the girls back, I know that it's not gonna change my life in that way… But just to think well, you know, you've put some kind of wrong right. I…I need some kind of conclusion to it now.

STEPHEN: I don't think it will ever come out, the full, the full story y'know. And again it's only thanks to likes of yourselves, young people getting interested in it and putting on something like this that'll keep the legend going. People y'know, whoever they are will fight in-justice. There's always someone who will fight injustice. So no, I don't think it will ever end.

Music – 'Power of Love' – Frankie Goes to Hollywood. Projected images of faces of Michael Kelly, Sarah Hicks, Vicki Hicks and Kevin Williams, then names of the 96 victims followed by dedication.

'This performance is dedicated to the 96 men, women and children who lost their lives at Hillsborough and the many thousands more that have been affected by the tragedy.'

'Thank You for The Days' – Kirsty MacColl.

Using *Beyond Hillsborough* in the Classroom

With motions in place for all young people on Merseyside to learn about the Hillsborough tragedy to 'ensure all future generations know the truth of what happened on that day' [1] it is hoped that this play may enable teachers to share first-hand accounts with young people to develop their knowledge and understanding. Here are a few suggestions for how this could be tackled in the classroom.

WAYS IN

Consider: EMPATHY / RESILIENCE / TOLERANCE

Initial Research Task
(This could be presented via PowerPoint/poster/collage/oral presentation/news report.)

Discover the 'who/what/where/when/why' circumstances surrounding the Hillsborough tragedy. To broaden students' research and present a higher level of challenge, have them consider the following questions: **have there ever been any other sporting disasters? What are the similarities/ differences?**

Show Jimmy McGovern's Drama Documentary, 'Hillsborough'
(An accessible way in for students at GCSE and above.)

As a follow-up exercise, ask students to consider if:

• advances in technology have improved public safety
• what safety precautions are taken at football matches/concerts /festivals today, and how might safety be improved further in the future?

(Students could work in small teams to design a futuristic 'safe space' for an event/football match/concert, etc, they could consider how technology could be used to enhance safety further – use of apps/monitoring systems/ignage etc, and present their design ideas to the class).

Read Beyond Hillsborough

Before reading the play, students could devise questions aimed at deepening their understanding; this may include some of the questions below, as the script is read students note their answers in preparation for class discussion.

- Why do you think this play was written?

- What do you think the main message of the play is?

- How did the play make you feel?

- What did you find most surprising/shocking/upsetting/ confusing?

- Why do you think the play is set in the present day?

- Did the play make you think about anything differently?

- Do young people need to know about a tragedy that happened many years ago?

- What does the term justice mean/what does it mean to the families and survivors?

- Why do you think family members and survivors fought for so long?

- Has there ever been a time when you have 'stood up' for something you believe in?

Research

Each of the support groups are represented in the play. Research the Hillsborough Family Support Group, Hillsborough Justice Campaign, Hope for Hillsborough further. What are the similarities and differences between each of the groups?

Exploring Themes

Divide the class into small groups of about 4 or 5 pupils. Then ask them to create tableaux (freeze frames/still images) to show the following themes: Justice, Injustice, Corruption, Perseverance, Unity, Trust, Deception. Link back to the events of Hillsborough and consider how they would now represent the themes. Try to get groups to consider how they would move fluidly between images.

Empathy

Ask each student to take on the role of a character from the play. They are to write an imaginary letter or diary entry outlining their thoughts and feelings. They should consider who their character would write to and the purpose of the letter. Students may prepare to perform this as a monologue or read it to the class, encourage the class to evaluate how truthful, to the character, their witting is. To extend this exercise students could 'hot-seat' their characters by answering questions from the group in role.

Introduction to Verbatim

Ask students to conduct interviews with family and friends to discover what they know and think about the Hillsborough tragedy, students devise their own questions, record interviewees responses.

Dramatising the Interviews

Students select 1 or 2 lines which they feel best sums up their interviewees' perspective, the whole class spread out in the space and take up the exact position of their interviewee by standing or sitting using appropriate posture. When the teacher points to a student they speak their interviewees' line(s) remembering to add pauses, sighs, hesitations as accurately as possible. This is repeated until all students have participated, they must remember the sequence, this time they must aim to overlap slightly so there is no pause between speakers, they may also explore the effect if everyone spoke at the same time. Perhaps split the group into 2 and allow them to watch the scene, which characters would we like to hear more from, do any characters have completely opposite ideas, how far does their research reflect public perceptions of the tragedy? How could the scene be developed further, could film footage/news reports be incorporated into the scene?

Finding the Students' Voice

Ask students to write a short paragraph to express their feelings about the Hillsborough tragedy by responding to the sentence 'what Hillsborough means to me'. Have them walk into the space and speak their words out loud. Blocking this as a piece of theatre is dramatic in itself but is particularly poignant for the class to reflect on at the end of the project.

Suggested Reading / Sources

The Day of the Hillsborough Disaster
R Taylor, A Ward, T Newburn

Hillsborough: The Truth
Professor Phil Scraton

The Nightmare of Hillsborough
Mike Bartram

The Hillsborough Stadium Disaster
Home Office

Hillsborough.independent.gov.uk

www.hfsg.co.uk

www.contrast.org/hillsborough

www.hopeforhillsborough.piczo.com

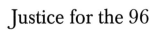

Justice for the 96

Printed in the USA
CPSIA information can be obtained
at www.ICGtesting.com
LVHW020942171024
794056LV00003B/906

9 781783 191345